Yes, But

by Kana Riley
illustrated by
Steven Guarnaccia

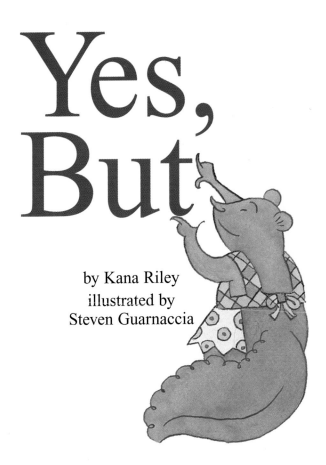

Scott Foresman

Editorial Offices: Glenview, Illinois • New York, New York
Sales Offices: Reading, Massachusetts • Duluth, Georgia
Glenview, Illinois • Carrollton, Texas • Menlo Park, California

Squirrel had a new home.
"Oh, dear," she said.
"I hope my friends like it.
I cannot wait to show them."

Along came Crow.
"Come in," said Squirrel.
"Do you like my new home?"

Crow took a look around.
"Yes," said Crow.
"But I have an idea.
Let me show you."

Crow pushed.
Crow pulled.
Crow put things up high.
"Now it looks great!" he said.

Along came Mouse.

"Come in," said Squirrel.

"Do you like my new home?"

Mouse took a look around.
"Yes," said Mouse.
"But I have an idea.
Let me show you."

Mouse pushed.
Mouse pulled.
Mouse put things down low.
"Now it looks great!" he said.

Along came Spider.

"Come in," said Squirrel.

"Do you like my new home?"

Spider took a look around.
"Yes," said Spider.
"But I have an idea.
Let me show you."

Spider pushed.
Spider pulled.
Spider moved things all around.
"Now it looks great!" she said.

Squirrel looked at her home.
"Now I don't like it," she said.
"But I have an idea!"

She called Crow.
She called Mouse.
She called Spider.

"Pull it here," Squirrel said.

"Push it there," she said.

"Now it looks great!" said Squirrel.